Table Of Contents

Chapter 1: Introduction to Social Media Crisis Management

Understanding Social Media Crisis Management

In today's digital age, social media has become a powerful tool that can greatly impact the reputation and image of public figures, brands, and organizations. With millions of active users and the ability to instantly reach a global audience, social media platforms have the potential to amplify both positive and negative messages. This subchapter, titled "Understanding Social Media Crisis Management," aims to provide public relations managers, social media managers, influencers, entrepreneurs, and digital marketing managers with valuable insights and strategies to effectively navigate and mitigate crises on social media platforms.

The subchapter begins by emphasizing the importance of understanding the dynamics of social media crises. It delves into the potential triggers and common scenarios that can lead to a crisis, such as offensive posts, negative reviews, data breaches, or viral controversies. By comprehending these triggers, public figures can better anticipate and prepare for potential crises, enabling them to respond swiftly and effectively.

The content then moves on to discuss damage control tactics for public figures on social media platforms. It highlights the significance of monitoring online conversations and mentions, as well as the importance of having a well-defined crisis management plan in place. The subchapter explores various strategies for handling crises, such as acknowledging the issue, apologizing if necessary, and providing transparent and timely updates. It also emphasizes the need to tailor the response based on the severity and nature of the crisis, as well as the target audience.

Furthermore, the subchapter delves into the role of social media influencers and entrepreneurs in crisis management. It provides insights on how influencers can protect their personal brand during a crisis and shares tips for entrepreneurs on maintaining their reputation in the face of negative feedback or online attacks. It also explores the ethical considerations and potential legal ramifications that public figures, influencers, and brands should be aware of when managing a crisis on social media platforms.

In conclusion, "Understanding Social Media Crisis Management" equips public relations managers, social media managers, influencers, entrepreneurs, and digital marketing managers with essential knowledge and strategies to effectively handle crises on social media platforms. By understanding the triggers, implementing damage control tactics, and navigating the unique challenges of social media, public figures can protect their reputation, maintain public trust, and emerge stronger from any crisis they encounter.

Importance of Effective Crisis Management for Public Figures

In today's digital age, where social media platforms have become the primary means of communication, public figures face an increased risk of encountering crises that can tarnish their reputation within seconds. This subchapter explores the significance of effective crisis management for public figures and provides invaluable strategies to navigate through these challenging situations.

Public relations managers, social media managers, influencers, entrepreneurs, and digital marketing managers must understand the potential consequences of a crisis and the impact it can have on a public figure's personal brand and professional endeavors. A crisis can emerge from various scenarios such as controversial statements, leaked private information, or negative public sentiment. Thus, having a proactive approach to crisis management is crucial.

One of the key reasons why effective crisis management is vital for public figures is the ability to mitigate damage. Social media platforms provide a powerful tool for spreading information rapidly, both positive and negative. Without proper management, a crisis can escalate quickly, leading to widespread negative publicity and long-lasting reputational damage. Therefore, public figures need to be equipped with damage control tactics specifically tailored for social media platforms.

Furthermore, effective crisis management allows public figures to maintain their credibility and trustworthiness. When a crisis occurs, the public expects transparency, accountability, and swift action. By addressing the crisis promptly and sincerely, public figures can preserve their credibility and rebuild trust with their audience. Failure to handle a crisis appropriately can result in alienating followers, loss of endorsements, and a damaged personal brand.

Public figures also need to understand the importance of social media crisis management as a means of protecting their professional endeavors. Whether they are entrepreneurs or influencers, their success often relies on their reputation and the perception of their audience. A poorly managed crisis can lead to lost business opportunities, reduced partnerships, and a decline in market value.

In conclusion, effective crisis management is of utmost importance for public figures in today's digital era. Public relations managers, social media managers, influencers, entrepreneurs, and digital marketing managers must be well-versed in damage control tactics specifically tailored for social media platforms. By effectively managing crises, public figures can mitigate damage, maintain credibility and trustworthiness, and protect their professional endeavors. This subchapter provides invaluable strategies for navigating through crises and serves as a comprehensive guide for anyone involved in managing the reputation of public figures on social media platforms.

Overview of Social Media Platforms and their Impact on Public Figures

Social media platforms have revolutionized the way public figures communicate and engage with their audience. With the rise of platforms such as Facebook, Twitter, Instagram, and YouTube, public figures now have direct access to millions of followers, allowing them to share their thoughts, ideas, and personal experiences instantly. However, this unprecedented level of accessibility comes with its own set of challenges and risks.

This subchapter will provide an in-depth overview of the various social media platforms and their impact on public figures. It aims to guide public relations managers, social media managers, influencers, entrepreneurs, and digital marketing managers in understanding the dynamics of these platforms and how to navigate them effectively during times of crisis.

The chapter will begin by examining the most popular social media platforms and their unique features. It will cover the strengths and weaknesses of platforms like Facebook, Twitter, Instagram, and YouTube, including their reach, engagement possibilities, and potential risks. This section will help readers identify the platforms that best suit their objectives and target audience.

Next, the subchapter will delve into the impact of social media on public figures. It will explore how these platforms have democratized fame and reshaped the relationship between public figures and their fans. The chapter will discuss the benefits of using social media as a public figure, such as increased visibility, direct communication, and personal branding. However, it will also highlight the potential pitfalls, such as privacy invasion, cyberbullying, and reputation damage.

The subchapter will then shift its focus to damage control tactics for public figures on social media platforms. It will provide practical strategies for managing crises, handling negative feedback, and mitigating reputational damage. The chapter will emphasize the importance of transparency, authenticity, and timely response in navigating social media crises effectively.

Lastly, the subchapter will offer case studies and real-life examples of public figures who have successfully managed social media crises. It will analyze their strategies, highlight key takeaways, and provide actionable insights for readers to implement in their own crisis management efforts.

Overall, this subchapter aims to equip public relations managers, social media managers, influencers, entrepreneurs, and digital marketing managers with a comprehensive understanding of social media platforms and their impact on public figures. By mastering the dynamics of these platforms and implementing effective damage control tactics, public figures can maintain their reputation, engage their audience, and thrive in the digital age.

Chapter 2: Preparing for a Social Media Crisis

Identifying Potential Crisis Triggers on Social Media

In today's digital age, social media has become an integral part of our daily lives. Public figures, influencers, entrepreneurs, and brands rely heavily on these platforms to connect with their audience and build their online presence. However, with great power comes great responsibility, and the potential for a crisis to unfold on social media is always present. As a public relations manager, social media manager, or digital marketing manager, it is crucial to be proactive in identifying potential crisis triggers on these platforms to effectively implement damage control tactics.

The first step in crisis management is being aware of the factors that can trigger a crisis on social media. One of the most common triggers is negative customer feedback or complaints. Due to the ease of sharing opinions on social media, a single disgruntled customer can quickly escalate into a full-blown crisis if not addressed promptly and effectively. Monitoring social media channels for any signs of dissatisfaction or negative sentiment is essential to nip potential crises in the bud.

Another trigger to watch out for is controversial or offensive content. Public figures and influencers must be cautious about the content they share or endorse, as it can potentially offend or alienate their audience. Regularly reviewing and auditing the content being shared on social media platforms can help identify any potential triggers and allow for adjustments or removal before they become crisis incidents.

Additionally, keeping an eye on trending topics and hashtags is vital. What may seem like an innocent hashtag or trending topic at first glance could turn into a PR nightmare if it is associated with controversial or sensitive subjects.

Being proactive in staying informed about trending conversations and understanding the context behind them can help public figures and brands avoid unintentional involvement in potential crises.

Utilizing social media monitoring tools can greatly assist in identifying potential crisis triggers. These tools allow for real-time tracking of brand mentions, sentiment analysis, and social media conversations related to the public figure or brand. By setting up alerts and monitoring relevant keywords, public relations managers and social media managers can quickly detect any emerging crisis and take immediate action.

In conclusion, being proactive in identifying potential crisis triggers on social media is crucial for public figures, influencers, entrepreneurs, and brands. By monitoring social media channels, auditing content, staying informed about trending topics, and utilizing social media monitoring tools, public relations managers, social media managers, and digital marketing managers can effectively implement damage control tactics and minimize the impact of potential crises on their clients or organizations.

Creating a Crisis Management Plan for Public Figures

In today's digital age, public figures are more vulnerable than ever to facing crises on social media platforms. The power of social media can both elevate their status and quickly bring them down. As a public relations manager, social media manager, influencer, entrepreneur, or digital marketing manager, it is crucial to have a well-thought-out crisis management plan in place to effectively handle any potential damage.

The first step in creating a crisis management plan for public figures is to anticipate potential crises and identify the most likely scenarios. This could include negative press, controversial statements, leaked personal information, or even false rumors. By understanding the possible triggers, you can develop strategies to mitigate their impact.

One of the key damage control tactics for public figures on social media platforms is to closely monitor their online presence. Regularly track mentions, comments, and discussions surrounding the public figure to identify any emerging issues or negative sentiment. This proactive approach allows for swift response and containment before a minor issue escalates into a full-blown crisis.

Another crucial aspect of crisis management is establishing clear lines of communication. Develop a network of trusted individuals who can act as spokespersons during a crisis. This team should include public relations professionals, legal advisors, and social media managers who can craft a consistent and strategic response. By having a designated crisis management team in place, public figures can ensure a unified and well-coordinated approach.

Additionally, public figures must be prepared to issue a timely and genuine apology if necessary. Admitting mistakes, taking responsibility, and outlining steps for improvement can help rebuild trust and minimize the long-term damage caused by a crisis. This is especially important in a world where social media users demand transparency and authenticity.

Finally, it is essential to constantly evaluate and update the crisis management plan. Social media platforms and trends evolve rapidly, and public figures must stay ahead of the curve. Regularly review and adapt the plan to address emerging challenges and incorporate lessons learned from past experiences.

In conclusion, public figures must be proactive in creating a crisis management plan to effectively navigate the ever-changing landscape of social media. By anticipating potential crises, closely monitoring online presence, establishing clear communication channels, issuing timely apologies, and continuously updating the plan, public figures can protect their reputation and mitigate the damage caused by social media crises.

Developing a Crisis Communication Team

In today's digital age, where information spreads like wildfire across social media platforms, public figures must be prepared to handle potential crises that may arise. It is no longer a matter of if a crisis will occur, but when. Thus, having a well-equipped crisis communication team is crucial for effective damage control.

Public relations managers, social media managers, influencers, entrepreneurs, and digital marketing managers must understand the importance of developing a crisis communication team. This subchapter will delve into the strategies and tactics required to build an efficient crisis communication team that can handle any social media crisis.

First and foremost, assembling the right team is essential. Identify individuals within your organization who possess the necessary skills and expertise to manage crises effectively. These team members should have a thorough understanding of social media platforms, crisis management techniques, and public relations strategies. They should be quick thinkers, adaptable, and capable of handling high-pressure situations.

Once you have identified your crisis communication team members, it is crucial to establish clear roles and responsibilities. Each team member should understand their specific duties and know how to collaborate effectively. This will ensure a coordinated and efficient response during a crisis.

Training and preparation are paramount when it comes to crisis management. Conduct regular drills and simulations to test your team's ability to handle different crisis scenarios. This will help identify any gaps in their knowledge or skills and allow for improvement before an actual crisis occurs.

In addition to training, staying up to date with the latest social media trends and platforms is vital. Your crisis communication team must be well-versed in the various social media platforms and the potential risks and challenges they present. This knowledge will enable them to respond promptly and appropriately during a crisis.

Lastly, establish a clear line of communication within your crisis communication team and ensure that all team members are aware of the reporting structure. This will facilitate effective decision-making and streamline the overall crisis management process.

In conclusion, developing a crisis communication team is a critical component of any public figure's social media crisis management strategy. By assembling the right team, defining roles and responsibilities, providing training and preparation, staying updated on social media trends, and establishing clear communication channels, public relations managers, social media managers, influencers, entrepreneurs, and digital marketing managers can effectively navigate and mitigate crises on social media platforms. A well-prepared crisis communication team is the key to successful damage control and maintaining a positive public image.

Establishing Monitoring and Alert Systems

In today's digital age, public figures face unique challenges in managing their online presence. With the increasing popularity and influence of social media platforms, the potential for a crisis to occur is higher than ever before. Therefore, it is crucial for public figures to establish effective monitoring and alert systems to mitigate and respond to any potential damage swiftly and efficiently.

Public relations managers, social media managers, influencers, entrepreneurs, and digital marketing managers play a vital role in safeguarding the reputation and brand image of public figures on social media platforms. This subchapter will provide valuable strategies and tactics for establishing monitoring and alert systems to effectively manage social media crises.

The first step in establishing an effective monitoring system is to identify the key platforms where the public figure has a significant presence. These platforms may include popular social media networks such as Facebook, Twitter, Instagram, YouTube, and LinkedIn. By monitoring these platforms regularly, public relations managers and social media managers can stay informed about any potential crisis or negative sentiment that may arise.

To streamline the monitoring process, public figures can utilize social media listening tools and software. These tools allow for real-time monitoring of social media platforms, enabling the team to track mentions, comments, and trends associated with the public figure. By harnessing the power of technology, the team can quickly identify and address any potential crisis before it escalates.

In addition to monitoring, establishing an alert system is crucial for timely crisis response. Public relations managers and social media managers should set up alerts for specific keywords, phrases, or mentions associated with the public figure. This proactive approach ensures that the team is alerted whenever a potential crisis or negative sentiment arises, allowing them to respond swiftly and effectively.

Furthermore, public figures should consider creating a crisis response plan that outlines the roles and responsibilities of each team member during a social media crisis. This plan should include clear guidelines on how to handle different types of crises, as well as a step-by-step process for escalation and resolution.

By establishing monitoring and alert systems, public figures can effectively manage crises on social media platforms. Public relations managers, social media managers, influencers, entrepreneurs, and digital marketing managers play a critical role in implementing these systems to ensure the reputation and brand image of public figures remain intact in the face of potential damage.

Chapter 3: Proactive Strategies for Crisis Prevention

Building a Strong Online Presence and Personal Brand

In today's digital age, having a strong online presence and personal brand is crucial, especially for public figures. Public relations managers, social media managers, influencers, entrepreneurs, and digital marketing managers need to understand the importance of building and maintaining a positive online image. This subchapter will delve into effective strategies for creating a solid online presence and personal brand, with a specific focus on damage control tactics for public figures on social media platforms.

Firstly, it is essential to establish a consistent and authentic personal brand across all social media platforms. This involves defining your values, passions, and expertise and showcasing them through engaging content. By consistently sharing valuable and relevant information, public figures can build trust and credibility with their audience. It is also crucial to ensure that the personal brand aligns with the public figure's overall image and goals.

Public figures should also be mindful of their online reputation and take proactive steps to protect it. Regularly monitoring and managing social media accounts is essential for identifying and addressing any potential issues or negative feedback promptly. Public relations and social media managers should develop a crisis management plan to handle any potential social media crises effectively. This plan should include designated spokespersons, clear communication protocols, and strategies for diffusing conflicts or controversies.

Engagement is another critical aspect of building a strong online presence. Public figures should actively interact with their audience, respond to comments, and participate in relevant discussions. By engaging with followers, public figures can establish a loyal community and strengthen their personal brand.

Moreover, public figures should leverage various social media platforms to expand their reach and influence. Each platform offers unique features and audience demographics, so it is crucial to tailor content based on the platform's characteristics. A well-rounded social media strategy will include a mix of text, images, videos, and live streaming content to cater to different preferences and engage a broader audience.

Lastly, public figures should continuously evaluate the effectiveness of their online presence and personal brand. Regularly analyzing metrics such as engagement, reach, and sentiment can provide valuable insights into the success of their strategies. Adjustments can be made accordingly to ensure continuous growth and improvement.

In conclusion, building a strong online presence and personal brand is crucial for public figures in today's digital landscape. By following the strategies outlined in this subchapter, public relations managers, social media managers, influencers, entrepreneurs, and digital marketing managers can create a positive and influential online image for public figures. By effectively managing their online reputation and engaging with their audience, public figures can mitigate potential social media crises and build a loyal and supportive community.

Crafting Engaging and Authentic Content

In the fast-paced world of social media, crafting engaging and authentic content is essential for public figures to maintain a positive online presence. This subchapter will explore the strategies that public relations managers, social media managers, influencers, entrepreneurs, and digital marketing managers can employ to ensure effective damage control on social media platforms.

Authenticity is the key to building a strong connection with your audience. In an era where people crave genuine experiences, public figures must present themselves in a real and relatable manner. This means embracing transparency and being honest about successes and failures. By sharing personal stories, insights, and struggles, public figures can humanize themselves, fostering a deeper connection with their followers.

Engagement is another crucial aspect of successful social media management. Public figures must actively engage with their audience by responding to comments, addressing concerns, and participating in discussions. This two-way communication builds trust, loyalty, and a sense of community. It is important to allocate time and resources to engage with followers genuinely.

To craft engaging content, public figures need to understand their target audience. Conducting thorough research and analyzing demographics, interests, and preferences will enable them to tailor content that resonates with their followers. Utilize this information to create content that is relevant, informative, and entertaining.

Public figures should consider incorporating different types of content formats to keep their audience engaged. Experiment with videos, live streams, infographics, and interactive posts to diversify your content strategy. This variety will not only keep your audience interested but also help you reach a wider demographic.

In times of crisis, public figures need to be prepared with a robust damage control strategy. This involves monitoring social media platforms for any negative feedback or backlash and addressing it promptly. Responding professionally, owning up to mistakes, and offering viable solutions can help in diffusing potentially damaging situations.

Furthermore, public figures should proactively build a positive online reputation through consistent and ethical practices. By consistently delivering valuable content, public figures can establish themselves as trusted sources in their respective niches.

Crafting engaging and authentic content on social media is an ongoing process. Public figures must continuously adapt to changing trends, platforms, and audience expectations. By staying true to their values, engaging with their followers, and proactively managing their online presence, public figures can successfully navigate crises and maintain a positive image in the digital world.

Engaging with Audiences and Building Trust

In today's digital age, social media platforms have become powerful tools for public figures to connect with their audiences. However, with great power comes great responsibility. Public figures must be prepared to handle any potential crisis that may arise on these platforms, which can quickly damage their reputation and credibility. This subchapter explores effective strategies for engaging with audiences and building trust, specifically tailored to public figures.

One of the fundamental aspects of engaging with audiences on social media is active listening. Public relations managers, social media managers, and influencers need to monitor conversations happening online, both about their clients and within their respective industries. By paying attention to what their audiences are saying, public figures can identify potential issues before they escalate into full-blown crises. Engaging in meaningful conversations, responding to comments and messages, and addressing concerns promptly not only shows that the public figure cares about their audience but also helps to build trust.

Another crucial aspect is authenticity. Audiences value genuine interactions and experiences. Public figures should strive to be authentic in their social media posts, sharing personal stories and insights that resonate with their followers. This authenticity helps to humanize the public figure and fosters a sense of trust and connection between them and their audience.

Building trust also requires transparency. Public figures should be open and honest about their actions and decisions. If a crisis occurs, they should address it head-on, providing a clear and honest explanation of the situation. By demonstrating transparency, public figures can maintain credibility and reassure their audiences that they are committed to resolving any issues that arise.

Furthermore, public figures should leverage social media platforms to showcase their expertise and provide value to their audience. Sharing educational content, industry insights, and behind-the-scenes glimpses can establish the public figure as a trusted source of information. This consistent sharing of valuable content helps to build credibility and fosters a loyal and engaged audience.

Lastly, public figures should establish a crisis management plan in advance. This plan should outline the steps to be taken in the event of a social media crisis, including who will be responsible for managing the situation, the key messages to convey, and the platforms to utilize for communication. By being prepared, public figures can respond swiftly and effectively, minimizing the potential damage to their reputation.

In conclusion, engaging with audiences and building trust on social media platforms is essential for public figures. By actively listening, being authentic, transparent, and providing value, public figures can foster strong connections with their audience. Additionally, having a well-defined crisis management plan in place ensures that public figures are prepared to handle any potential crises that may arise on social media platforms.

Monitoring Online Conversations and Sentiment Analysis

In today's digital era, social media platforms have become an integral part of our lives. Public figures, including celebrities, politicians, and entrepreneurs, often find themselves in the spotlight on these platforms. However, with great popularity comes great risk. Any wrong move or misstep can quickly escalate into a full-blown crisis, potentially tarnishing their reputation and causing significant damage.

To mitigate these risks and effectively manage social media crises, public relations managers, social media managers, and influencers must employ proactive strategies. One such strategy is monitoring online conversations and conducting sentiment analysis. This subchapter will delve into the importance of these tactics and how they can be utilized for damage control.

Monitoring online conversations involves keeping a close eye on social media platforms, news websites, blogs, and forums to identify any potential issues or negative discussions related to public figures. By actively monitoring these platforms, PR managers can promptly address emerging problems and take appropriate action to prevent further escalation. This includes responding to negative comments, correcting misinformation, and engaging with users to provide accurate information.

In addition to monitoring conversations, sentiment analysis is a powerful tool that helps gauge the public's perception and sentiment towards a public figure during a crisis. It involves analyzing social media posts, comments, and other online interactions to determine whether the sentiment is positive, negative, or neutral. By understanding the prevailing sentiment, PR managers can tailor their crisis management strategies accordingly.

Sentiment analysis can be automated using various software and tools that employ natural language processing algorithms. These tools can analyze vast amounts of data in real-time, providing valuable insights into public sentiment. This enables PR managers to make informed decisions and craft appropriate responses that resonate with the public.

Furthermore, sentiment analysis can help identify influential individuals or groups that are driving the negative sentiment. By identifying key opinion leaders, PR managers can engage in proactive outreach to address concerns, clarify misconceptions, and potentially turn negative sentiment into positive advocacy.

In conclusion, monitoring online conversations and conducting sentiment analysis are essential damage control tactics for public figures on social media platforms. By actively monitoring conversations and analyzing sentiment, PR managers can proactively address emerging issues, correct misinformation, and engage with the public effectively. These strategies enable public figures to maintain their reputation and manage crises in a more informed and efficient manner.

Chapter 4: Reactive Strategies for Crisis Response

Identifying and Assessing Social Media Crises

In today's digital age, social media platforms have become powerful tools for public figures to connect with their audience, build their brand, and share their message. However, with great power comes great responsibility, and it is crucial for public figures to be prepared for potential social media crises that can damage their reputation and brand. This subchapter will delve into the strategies and tactics that public relations managers, social media managers, influencers, entrepreneurs, and digital marketing managers can employ to identify and assess social media crises, as well as implement effective damage control tactics.

The first step in handling a social media crisis is to identify it early. Public figures need to be vigilant and constantly monitor their social media channels for any signs of trouble. This can include negative comments, backlash, rumors, or any other form of online criticism. By proactively identifying potential crises, public figures can take immediate action to mitigate the damage.

Once a crisis has been identified, it is crucial to assess the situation accurately. This involves conducting a thorough analysis of the situation, understanding the root cause, and determining the potential impact on the public figure's reputation and brand. Public relations managers, social media managers, and influencers should work together to gather information, monitor the online sentiment, and assess the severity of the crisis. This will provide the foundation for an effective crisis management strategy.

When it comes to damage control tactics for public figures on social media platforms, transparency and authenticity are key. Public figures should respond promptly, openly, and honestly to address the crisis. This includes acknowledging the issue, apologizing if necessary, and providing a clear plan of action to rectify the situation. Moreover, it is essential to engage with the audience, listen to their concerns, and provide regular updates to rebuild trust.

Additionally, public figures should leverage their existing relationships with their audience and influencers within their niche to counteract the negative impact of the crisis. By mobilizing their supporters, public figures can amplify positive messages, debunk rumors, and regain control of the narrative.

In conclusion, social media crises can pose significant threats to public figures' reputation and brand. However, by identifying and assessing these crises early and implementing effective damage control tactics, public relations managers, social media managers, influencers, entrepreneurs, and digital marketing managers can navigate through these challenges and emerge stronger. This subchapter serves as a comprehensive guide to help professionals in these roles develop strategies to handle social media crises and protect the public figures they represent.

Developing Crisis Communication Frameworks

In the fast-paced digital age, where information spreads like wildfire, public figures are increasingly vulnerable to social media crises that can damage their reputation and credibility. To effectively navigate these challenges, public relations managers, social media managers, influencers, entrepreneurs, and digital marketing managers must develop robust crisis communication frameworks. This subchapter explores the importance of such frameworks and presents key strategies for damage control tactics on social media platforms.

A crisis communication framework serves as a roadmap for managing and mitigating the impact of a social media crisis. It ensures that public figures respond promptly, effectively, and consistently, while maintaining transparency and trust. This framework encompasses various elements, including pre-crisis planning, crisis response protocols, and post-crisis evaluation.

Pre-crisis planning is critical for any public figure. It involves conducting a risk assessment to identify potential crises and their likelihood. Understanding the target audience, social media platforms, and potential influencers within the niche is essential for developing an effective crisis communication plan. Public figures should establish clear guidelines and protocols for their social media teams, outlining roles, responsibilities, and communication channels during a crisis.

During a crisis, the response should be swift and empathetic. It is crucial to have a designated crisis communication team that can monitor social media platforms, identify potential crises, and respond promptly. The team should be well-versed in the public figure's messaging and brand voice to ensure consistency. Public figures should adopt a proactive approach, issuing public statements, acknowledging mistakes, and offering transparent explanations. It is vital to monitor public sentiment, engage with the audience, and address their concerns promptly. Utilizing social media listening tools can help identify emerging trends and gauge public sentiment in real-time.

Post-crisis evaluation is equally important for continuous improvement. Public figures should conduct a thorough analysis of the crisis response, identifying strengths and weaknesses. This evaluation can help refine the crisis communication framework and identify areas for improvement. Public figures should also monitor the long-term impact of the crisis on their reputation and take corrective actions if necessary.

In conclusion, developing crisis communication frameworks is essential for public figures to effectively manage social media crises. By following pre-crisis planning, crisis response protocols, and post-crisis evaluation, public relations managers, social media managers, influencers, entrepreneurs, and digital marketing managers can employ damage control tactics that protect the reputation and credibility of public figures on social media platforms.

Crafting Timely and Effective Crisis Messages

In today's digital age, where social media platforms dominate the communication landscape, public figures are more susceptible than ever to crises that can damage their reputation in an instant. Public relations managers, social media managers, influencers, entrepreneurs, and digital marketing managers must be equipped with the necessary skills to handle and mitigate such crises effectively. This subchapter aims to provide valuable insights and strategies for crafting timely and effective crisis messages in the realm of social media crisis management.

When a crisis strikes, time is of the essence. Public figures need to respond promptly to demonstrate their commitment to addressing the issue at hand. Crafting a timely crisis message requires a comprehensive understanding of the situation, including its causes, potential consequences, and the sentiment of the audience. Public relations managers must gather all relevant information and consult with the relevant stakeholders to ensure the message is accurate and aligns with the brand's values.

An effective crisis message should be concise, transparent, and empathetic. It is crucial to acknowledge the issue, take responsibility, and express genuine concern for those affected. Public figures should demonstrate their commitment to finding a solution and preventing similar crises in the future. It is essential to avoid defensive or dismissive language, as this can further exacerbate the situation and damage the public figure's reputation.

Moreover, crisis messages should be tailored to the specific social media platform on which they are shared. Each platform has its unique characteristics and audience expectations. Public relations managers and social media managers must adapt their messages accordingly to ensure maximum impact and reach. Utilizing visuals, such as infographics or videos, can also enhance the message's effectiveness by making it more engaging and shareable.

In addition to crafting timely and effective crisis messages, public figures must also utilize damage control tactics on social media platforms. This includes monitoring mentions and conversations related to the crisis, engaging with the audience in a respectful and empathetic manner, and addressing any misinformation or rumors promptly. Furthermore, public figures should leverage social media analytics to track the impact of their crisis messages and adjust their strategies accordingly.

Overall, effective crisis message crafting is a crucial skill for public figures in today's digital world. By being proactive, transparent, and empathetic, public relations managers, social media managers, influencers, entrepreneurs, and digital marketing managers can navigate and mitigate crises successfully, preserving their reputation and maintaining the trust of their audience.

Leveraging Influencers and Advocates for Support

In the ever-evolving landscape of social media, public figures face a constant risk of encountering a crisis that can potentially damage their reputation and credibility. These crises can be triggered by a variety of factors, including negative public sentiment, false allegations, or even a simple misstep in communication. However, with the right strategies in place, public figures can effectively manage such crises and emerge stronger than ever.

One powerful tactic in damage control for public figures on social media platforms is leveraging influencers and advocates for support. These individuals have amassed a significant following and possess the ability to influence public opinion. By working with them, public figures can tap into their credibility and reach to counteract negative narratives and rebuild their reputation.

Public relations managers and social media managers play a crucial role in identifying and collaborating with relevant influencers and advocates. They need to conduct comprehensive research to find individuals who align with the values and interests of the public figure they represent. This ensures that the partnership appears genuine and authentic, thereby increasing the likelihood of a positive reception from the audience.

Entrepreneurs and digital marketing managers can also benefit from this strategy by leveraging influencers and advocates to mitigate potential crises. By proactively building relationships with these influential individuals, they can create a network of support that can be mobilized in times of need. This network acts as a safety net, ready to amplify positive messages and counteract any negative publicity.

When engaging influencers and advocates, it is crucial to establish a mutually beneficial relationship. Public figures should provide these individuals with exclusive access, behind-the-scenes content, or even financial incentives, in exchange for their support during a crisis. Additionally, public figures should provide them with the necessary information and resources to accurately represent their brand and message.

Collaborating with influencers and advocates during a crisis allows public figures to leverage their influence to shape public perception and control the narrative. By strategically disseminating positive messaging through these trusted channels, it becomes possible to regain trust and credibility in the eyes of the public.

In conclusion, leveraging influencers and advocates for support is a crucial component of social media crisis management for public figures. Public relations managers, social media managers, influencers, entrepreneurs, and digital marketing managers must recognize the power of these individuals in shaping public opinion. By establishing authentic partnerships, providing exclusive benefits, and effectively communicating their brand message, public figures can successfully navigate crises and emerge stronger than before.

Chapter 5: Managing Different Types of Social Media Crises

Handling Rumors and Misinformation

In today's digital age, rumors and misinformation can spread like wildfire, especially on social media platforms. Public figures, including influencers, entrepreneurs, and politicians, find themselves particularly vulnerable to the damaging effects of false information. As a public relations manager, social media manager, or digital marketing manager, it is crucial to have effective damage control tactics in place to mitigate the impact of rumors and misinformation on your client's reputation and public image.

1. Assess the Situation: The first step in handling rumors and misinformation is to assess the situation. Determine the source, the extent of the spread, and the potential harm it may cause to your client's reputation. This will help you formulate an appropriate response strategy.

2. Respond Swiftly and Transparently: One of the most important aspects of managing rumors and misinformation is to respond swiftly and transparently. Address the issue publicly, acknowledging the concerns and providing accurate information to counter the false claims. Use social media platforms to disseminate the correct information and engage in open dialogue with your audience.

3. Monitor Social Media Channels: Keep a close eye on social media channels to identify new rumors or misinformation as they arise. Utilize social listening tools to track mentions and keywords related to your client's name or brand. By staying vigilant, you can quickly identify and respond to false information before it gains traction.

4. Establish Relationships with Influencers: Collaborating with influencers can be a powerful tool in combating rumors and misinformation. Engage with

influencers who have a strong following and credibility in your client's industry. Encourage them to share accurate information and debunk false claims. Influencers can play a vital role in reestablishing trust and credibility for your client.

5. Provide Evidence and Facts: When countering rumors and misinformation, ensure that your responses are backed by evidence and facts. Use credible sources to support your claims and provide concrete evidence to debunk false information. This will help build trust and credibility with your audience and provide them with accurate information to make informed decisions.

6. Monitor the Impact: Continuously monitor the impact of your response strategy. Analyze engagement rates, sentiment analysis, and brand mentions to gauge the effectiveness of your efforts. Adjust your tactics accordingly to ensure maximum damage control.

In conclusion, handling rumors and misinformation on social media platforms requires a proactive and strategic approach. By assessing the situation, responding swiftly and transparently, monitoring social media channels, leveraging influencers, providing evidence, and monitoring the impact, public relations managers, social media managers, and influencers can effectively manage and mitigate the damaging effects of false information on their client's reputation and public image.

Addressing Negative Publicity and Online Attacks

In today's digital age, public figures are more vulnerable than ever to negative publicity and online attacks. With the power of social media, news spreads rapidly, and public figures find themselves at the center of storms, facing backlash, and dealing with potential reputation damage. However, with effective social media crisis management strategies, public figures can navigate these challenging situations while minimizing the impact on their personal brand and reputation.

This subchapter aims to provide public relations managers, social media managers, influencers, entrepreneurs, and digital marketing managers with valuable insights and damage control tactics for handling negative publicity and online attacks on social media platforms.

1. Monitoring and Identifying Potential Issues:
Public figures must proactively monitor their social media platforms, news outlets, and other online platforms to identify potential issues before they escalate. Utilizing social listening tools and staying up-to-date with the latest trends and conversations can help public figures anticipate and address any negative publicity.

2. Swift Response and Authenticity:
When faced with negative publicity or online attacks, public figures should respond swiftly and authentically. Ignoring or deleting comments can often exacerbate the situation, leading to further backlash. Instead, public figures should acknowledge the concerns raised, provide factual information, and express empathy to demonstrate their commitment to addressing the issue.

3. Engage with Influencers and Supporters:
Public figures can leverage the support of influencers and engage with their loyal fan base to counter negative publicity. Collaborating with influential figures who align with their personal brand can help shift the narrative and garner positive attention. Additionally, public figures should actively respond to positive comments and engage with supporters to maintain a strong online presence.

4. Crisis Communication Plan:
Having a crisis communication plan in place is crucial for public figures. This plan should outline the steps to be taken in the event of a crisis, including designating spokespersons, preparing key messages, and determining the appropriate channels for communication. By having a well-structured plan, public figures can respond effectively and minimize the impact of negative publicity.

5. Seek Legal Advice if Necessary:
In severe cases of online attacks or false accusations, public figures should consider seeking legal advice. Legal professionals specializing in online reputation management can help public figures navigate legal challenges and protect their personal brand.

In conclusion, negative publicity and online attacks can be damaging to public figures' reputation, but with the right strategies, it is possible to manage these crises effectively. By actively monitoring, responding authentically, engaging with influencers and supporters, having a crisis communication plan, and seeking legal advice when necessary, public figures can address negative publicity while maintaining their personal brand and reputation on social media platforms.

Dealing with Customer Complaints and Dissatisfaction

In the fast-paced world of social media, public figures often find themselves at the center of attention, both for positive and negative reasons. While these platforms offer great opportunities for engagement and brand building, they also pose significant challenges when it comes to managing customer complaints and dissatisfaction. In this subchapter, we will explore effective strategies and damage control tactics that public figures can employ to address and resolve customer issues on social media platforms.

1. Acknowledge and Respond Promptly: The first step in dealing with customer complaints is to acknowledge their concerns promptly. Public figures must understand the power of social media and the effect a quick response can have on diffusing a potentially volatile situation. Responding in a timely manner shows that you value your customers and are committed to resolving their issues.

2. Empathize and Apologize: When addressing customer complaints, it is crucial to empathize with their frustrations and offer a sincere apology for any

inconvenience caused. Public figures should remember that their reputation is at stake and a genuine apology can go a long way in restoring trust and goodwill.

3. Take the Conversation Offline: While it is important to address complaints publicly, public figures should aim to take the conversation offline as soon as possible. Providing a direct contact information or suggesting private messaging platforms allows for a more personalized and efficient resolution process.

4. Offer Solutions and Compensations: Public figures should provide tangible solutions to customer complaints. Whether it is a refund, replacement, or any other form of compensation, offering a resolution demonstrates your commitment to customer satisfaction.

5. Monitor and Learn: Public figures should actively monitor social media platforms for complaints and negative feedback. By keeping an eye on trends and recurring issues, you can identify areas for improvement and prevent future complaints.

6. Train and Empower Your Team: Public figures should ensure that their PR and social media teams are well-trained in handling customer complaints. Empowering your team with the knowledge and tools to address issues effectively will help maintain a positive brand image.

7. Learn from Success Stories: Public figures can learn from successful case studies of other brands and public figures who have effectively managed customer complaints on social media. Analyzing these success stories can provide valuable insights and inspiration for your own crisis management strategies.

By implementing these strategies and tactics, public figures can effectively manage customer complaints and dissatisfaction on social media platforms. Remember, in the digital age, customer satisfaction is paramount, and your response to complaints can make all the difference in preserving your reputation and maintaining positive relationships with your audience.

Responding to Legal and Ethical Issues

In today's digital age, social media has become an integral part of our lives, especially for public figures, influencers, entrepreneurs, and brands. However, with the immense power of social media comes great responsibility. Public figures are often faced with legal and ethical issues that can damage their reputation and impact their careers. It is crucial for public relations managers, social media managers, and digital marketing managers to be aware of the potential pitfalls and have strategies in place to effectively respond to these challenges.

One of the first steps in responding to legal and ethical issues on social media is to establish a comprehensive crisis management plan. This plan should outline the steps to be taken when faced with a crisis, including legal considerations and ethical guidelines. It is essential to proactively address potential issues and have a clear understanding of the laws and regulations governing social media platforms.

When a legal or ethical issue arises, it is important to respond promptly and transparently. Public figures should acknowledge the issue, take responsibility if necessary, and provide a clear plan for resolving the situation. Transparency builds trust and shows that the public figure is committed to addressing the issue head-on.

Public relations managers and social media managers should work closely with legal counsel to ensure that all responses are legally compliant. This includes understanding the laws surrounding defamation, privacy, intellectual property, and advertising. It is crucial to strike a balance between protecting the public figure's rights and addressing any legal concerns.

Furthermore, public figures should also consider the ethical implications of their actions on social media. They must be mindful of their impact on their audience and the wider society. Ethical guidelines should be established to guide their behavior on social media platforms, including guidelines on promoting diversity, inclusivity, and responsible marketing practices.

In addition to legal and ethical considerations, public figures should also employ damage control tactics to mitigate the impact of a crisis. This may include issuing public apologies, removing offensive content, and engaging with the affected parties to find a resolution. It is crucial to monitor the situation closely and respond promptly to any negative comments or backlash.

In conclusion, social media has become a powerful tool for public figures, influencers, entrepreneurs, and brands. However, with this power comes the responsibility to navigate legal and ethical issues effectively. By establishing a comprehensive crisis management plan, responding promptly and transparently, and working closely with legal counsel, public figures can effectively address legal and ethical challenges and protect their reputation on social media platforms.

Chapter 6: Engaging with the Public during a Crisis

Understanding the Importance of Transparency and Authenticity

In today's digital age, where information spreads at lightning speed, public figures must navigate the treacherous waters of social media with caution. Every action they take, every word they say, can have immediate and far-reaching consequences. This is why understanding the importance of transparency and authenticity is crucial for public figures, and why it should be a key component of any social media crisis management strategy.

Transparency is the foundation upon which trust is built. Public relations managers, social media managers, influencers, entrepreneurs, and digital marketing managers must recognize that their audience expects open and honest communication. By being transparent, public figures can establish credibility and maintain a positive image. It involves being forthright about intentions, disclosing conflicts of interest, and being open about any mistakes or missteps. Transparency helps to humanize public figures and allows their audience to relate to them on a more personal level.

Authenticity goes hand in hand with transparency. In a world where fake news and false narratives are rampant, being authentic is a powerful way to cut through the noise and build a genuine connection with the audience. Authenticity means staying true to oneself, having a consistent voice, and delivering content that aligns with one's values and beliefs. It involves sharing personal stories, expressing genuine emotions, and avoiding the temptation to present a polished, manufactured image.

Transparency and authenticity are not only ethical imperatives but also effective damage control tactics for public figures on social media platforms. When a crisis arises, such as a scandal or a controversy, these principles can help public figures regain control of the narrative and rebuild trust with their audience. By acknowledging the issue, taking responsibility, and addressing concerns openly and honestly, public figures can turn a crisis into an opportunity for growth and redemption.

For public relations managers, social media managers, influencers, entrepreneurs, and digital marketing managers, understanding the importance of transparency and authenticity is paramount. It not only helps to protect the reputation of the public figure but also strengthens the bond with their audience. By incorporating these principles into their social media crisis management strategies, they can navigate the turbulent waters of social media with confidence and resilience, ensuring the long-term success and sustainability of the public figure they represent.

In conclusion, transparency and authenticity are crucial elements for public figures to master in the realm of social media crisis management. By embracing these principles, public figures can build trust, establish credibility, and connect with their audience on a deeper level. In an era where reputation can be tarnished in an instant, the understanding and application of transparency and authenticity can be the difference between success and downfall for any public figure.

Choosing the Right Communication Channels

In today's digital age, social media has become an essential tool for public figures to connect with their audience and build their personal brands. However, with great power comes great responsibility, and the potential for social media crises is always lurking around the corner. As a public figure, it is crucial to have a well-defined strategy for crisis management, and choosing the right communication channels is a key component of that strategy.

When a crisis strikes on social media, time is of the essence. Therefore, it is vital for public relations managers, social media managers, influencers, entrepreneurs, and digital marketing managers to be well-versed in damage control tactics for public figures on social media platforms. The first step in effectively managing a crisis is selecting the most appropriate communication channels to address the issue promptly and efficiently.

One of the primary considerations when choosing the right communication channels is understanding your target audience. Different platforms attract different demographics and have distinct communication styles. Public figures must identify the platforms where their audience is most active and engaged. For example, if your target audience consists of young adults, platforms like Instagram and TikTok may be more effective than traditional ones like Facebook or LinkedIn.

Another crucial factor to consider when selecting communication channels is the nature of the crisis. Some crises can be resolved through a well-crafted statement or a carefully worded post, while others may require a more personal touch. For instance, if the crisis involves a misunderstanding or misinformation, addressing it publicly through a live video stream on platforms like Facebook or YouTube can help humanize the situation and foster trust among your audience.

Additionally, it is essential to leverage the strengths of each social media platform. Twitter, with its quick and concise format, is ideal for sharing real-time updates and responding to inquiries. Instagram, on the other hand, allows for more visual storytelling, making it suitable for rebuilding trust through behind-the-scenes content or personal reflections.

Ultimately, the key to choosing the right communication channels during a social media crisis lies in understanding your audience, tailoring your message to the nature of the crisis, and leveraging the unique strengths of each platform. By mastering these strategies, public figures can effectively navigate the treacherous waters of social media crises and emerge stronger than ever before.

Engaging with the Public through Social Media Platforms

In today's digital age, social media has become an integral part of our lives. It has not only revolutionized the way we connect and communicate with each other but has also emerged as a powerful tool for public figures to engage with their audience. However, with great power comes great responsibility. Public figures need to be vigilant and proactive in managing their social media presence, especially during times of crisis. This subchapter will delve into the strategies and tactics that can be employed by public figures to engage with the public effectively through social media platforms and mitigate any damage that may arise.

Public relations managers, social media managers, influencers, entrepreneurs, and digital marketing managers play a crucial role in ensuring the positive image and reputation of public figures on social media platforms. They must be well-versed in damage control tactics and equipped with the knowledge to navigate through challenging situations.

First and foremost, it is essential for public figures to maintain an active presence on social media platforms. Regularly posting engaging and relevant content will help build a loyal following and establish a relationship of trust with the audience. This will prove beneficial during times of crisis as the public will be more likely to listen and engage with the figure's perspective.

Secondly, public figures should be prepared to handle negative comments and feedback on social media. Timely responses to criticism can help defuse the situation and demonstrate that the figure is open to feedback and willing to address concerns. It is crucial to remain calm, professional, and empathetic when engaging with the public, as any aggressive or defensive behavior can further escalate the situation.

Moreover, public figures should leverage the power of storytelling on social media platforms. Sharing personal stories, experiences, and achievements can humanize the figure and create a deeper connection with the audience. This approach can help mitigate damage during a crisis by reminding the public of the figure's positive contributions and intentions.

Public figures should also consider utilizing influencers and brand ambassadors to amplify their message and reach a wider audience. Collaborating with influencers who align with the figure's values and beliefs can help disseminate positive content and counter any negative narratives circulating on social media.

Lastly, public figures must continually monitor their social media presence and stay updated with the latest trends and platforms. This will enable them to adapt their strategies accordingly and engage with the public effectively. Social media listening tools can be employed to track conversations, sentiment, and trends, allowing for proactive crisis management.

Engaging with the public through social media platforms is an art that requires careful planning, strategic thinking, and effective communication. By following the strategies and tactics discussed in this subchapter, public figures can effectively navigate through crises on social media and maintain a positive image in the eyes of their audience.

Handling Media and Press Inquiries during a Crisis

In the fast-paced world of social media, public figures are constantly under the scrutiny of the public eye. As a public relations manager, social media manager, influencer, entrepreneur, or digital marketing manager, it is crucial to be prepared for any crisis that may arise. One key aspect of crisis management is effectively handling media and press inquiries during such times.

During a crisis, the media plays a significant role in shaping public perception. It is essential to have a well-thought-out strategy in place to handle media and press inquiries promptly and effectively. Here are some damage control tactics for public figures on social media platforms:

1. Develop a Crisis Communication Plan: Before a crisis occurs, create a comprehensive crisis communication plan. This plan should outline key messages, designated spokespersons, and protocols for handling media inquiries. By having a plan in place, you can respond quickly and maintain control over the narrative.

2. Establish Relationships with Media: Building relationships with journalists and media outlets before a crisis occurs can be invaluable. Establishing trust and open lines of communication ensures that your message is accurately conveyed and provides an opportunity to share your perspective.

3. Respond Promptly and Transparently: When facing a crisis, it is essential to respond promptly to media inquiries. Ignoring or delaying a response can lead to speculation and damage the public's trust. Be transparent and provide accurate information to maintain credibility.

4. Prepare Key Messages: Craft key messages that clearly communicate your position and address the concerns of the public. These messages should be consistent across all communication channels, including social media platforms.

5. Train Spokespersons: Designate and train spokespersons who are adept at handling media inquiries. These individuals should be well-versed in the crisis communication plan and able to effectively convey key messages while remaining calm under pressure.

6. Monitor Social Media Channels: In today's digital age, social media platforms can amplify a crisis. Continuously monitor social media channels for any negative comments or misinformation and respond promptly to address concerns.

7. Be Proactive: In addition to responding to media inquiries, proactively share updates and information through press releases, social media posts, or targeted interviews. By taking control of the narrative, you can shape public perception and mitigate potential damage.

Remember, handling media and press inquiries during a crisis is a delicate and critical task. By implementing these damage control tactics for public figures on social media platforms, you can effectively manage crises and protect your reputation.

Chapter 7: Learning from Past Crises and Case Studies

Analyzing Real-life Crisis Situations Faced by Public Figures

In today's digital age, public figures are more vulnerable than ever before. With the rise of social media platforms, public figures, including celebrities, politicians, influencers, and entrepreneurs, face a constant risk of getting caught in a crisis situation that can damage their reputation and brand. To effectively manage and navigate these crises, public relations managers, social media managers, and digital marketing managers need to understand the complexities of real-life crisis situations faced by public figures.

This subchapter delves into the various crisis situations that public figures may encounter on social media platforms and provides insights into damage control tactics to mitigate the negative impact.

One common crisis situation faced by public figures is the spread of false information or rumors. In today's fast-paced social media environment, misinformation can spread like wildfire, leading to significant damage to a public figure's reputation. Public relations managers must be equipped with strategies to quickly identify and address false information, such as issuing statements, leveraging fact-checking organizations, or engaging with followers to debunk rumors.

Another crisis situation explored in this subchapter is the mishandling of sensitive topics or controversial statements. Public figures often find themselves in hot water due to a poorly worded tweet or an ill-advised comment. Social media managers must guide public figures on handling such situations with transparency and empathy, issuing apologies or clarifications when necessary, and utilizing social media platforms as a means to initiate meaningful conversations and bridge gaps.

Additionally, this subchapter examines crisis situations involving public figures who become embroiled in scandals or legal issues. Public relations managers must develop crisis management plans to address these situations promptly, including providing legal guidance, managing media inquiries, and taking appropriate actions to demonstrate accountability and responsibility.

Furthermore, the subchapter explores strategies for dealing with personal attacks, cyberbullying, or harassment targeted at public figures. Social media managers must implement robust monitoring systems to identify and address instances of online abuse swiftly. They must also work closely with influencers and entrepreneurs to establish online communities that promote positivity and support.

In conclusion, this subchapter provides valuable insights into the real-life crisis situations faced by public figures on social media platforms. Public relations managers, social media managers, and digital marketing managers will gain a deeper understanding of the complexities involved in managing crises and will be equipped with damage control tactics to safeguard the reputation and brand of public figures. By analyzing and learning from past crisis situations, professionals in these roles can effectively navigate the challenges posed by social media and protect the public image of their clients or organizations.

Extracting Lessons Learned and Best Practices

In the fast-paced world of social media, public figures often find themselves in the spotlight, facing potential crises that can damage their reputation and public image. Public relations managers, social media managers, influencers, entrepreneurs, and digital marketing managers need to be equipped with effective strategies for damage control on social media platforms. This subchapter, titled "Extracting Lessons Learned and Best Practices," aims to provide valuable insights and practical guidance on navigating social media crises successfully.

Lessons learned from past social media crises can serve as a powerful tool for public figures and their teams. By studying previous instances of damage control, they can identify common patterns, understand the consequences of specific actions, and develop informed strategies. This subchapter emphasizes the importance of conducting post-crisis analysis and extracting valuable lessons. It delves into case studies of both successful and unsuccessful crisis management, highlighting key takeaways for public figures.

Furthermore, understanding best practices in social media crisis management is crucial for public figures to proactively protect their reputation. This subchapter outlines a set of effective strategies and tactics that have proven successful in mitigating crises on various social media platforms. It covers the importance of monitoring online conversations, having a well-defined crisis communication plan, and training teams to respond promptly and professionally.

Additionally, this subchapter recognizes the unique challenges faced by public figures in managing social media crises. It offers practical advice on maintaining authenticity while navigating sensitive situations, leveraging the power of influencers and brand advocates to support crisis management efforts, and employing transparency as a strategic tool.

By combining lessons learned from past crises with best practices in social media crisis management, public relations managers, social media managers, influencers, entrepreneurs, and digital marketing managers can effectively safeguard their public image and reputation. This subchapter acts as a comprehensive guide, providing valuable insights and practical strategies for damage control tactics on social media platforms.

In conclusion, "Extracting Lessons Learned and Best Practices" is a subchapter that addresses the specific needs of public figures and their teams in managing social media crises. It offers valuable insights, case studies, and practical guidance to help public relations managers, social media managers, influencers, entrepreneurs, and digital marketing managers navigate challenging situations and protect their reputation in the digital age.

Case Studies of Successful Crisis Management in Social Media

In today's digital age, social media platforms have become a powerful tool for public figures to connect with their audience. However, with great power comes great responsibility. Public figures must be prepared to handle potential crises that can arise on these platforms. This subchapter explores successful case studies of crisis management in social media, providing valuable insights and strategies for public relations managers, social media managers, influencers, entrepreneurs, and digital marketing managers.

One notable case study is the crisis faced by a renowned fashion brand when a controversial advertisement sparked outrage on social media. The brand's social media team swiftly responded by issuing a sincere apology and acknowledging the mistake. They demonstrated transparency by explaining how the ad was created and assured their audience that they would take immediate action to rectify the situation. By actively engaging with their audience and addressing concerns, the brand was able to salvage its reputation and regain trust.

Another compelling case study involves a well-known celebrity who faced backlash due to an offensive comment made on a social media platform. The celebrity's crisis management team promptly issued a public apology on multiple platforms, ensuring maximum reach. They also demonstrated a commitment to change by engaging with organizations focused on the issue at hand and actively participating in educational initiatives. Through these actions, the celebrity successfully rebuilt their public image and used the crisis as an opportunity for growth and personal development.

In both case studies, the key to successful crisis management was the effective use of social media platforms to communicate with the audience. Public relations managers and social media managers played a crucial role in crafting and disseminating messages that were sincere, transparent, and empathetic. Additionally, influencers and entrepreneurs can learn from these case studies by understanding the importance of taking immediate action, engaging with their audience, and demonstrating a willingness to learn from mistakes.

Digital marketing managers can also benefit from studying these case studies as they highlight the significance of monitoring social media platforms and proactively addressing any potential crises. By developing a crisis management plan and staying prepared for unforeseen circumstances, public figures can effectively manage their online presence and mitigate any damage that may occur.

In conclusion, the case studies presented in this subchapter provide valuable insights into successful crisis management in social media for public figures. By understanding and implementing the damage control tactics discussed, public relations managers, social media managers, influencers, entrepreneurs, and digital marketing managers can navigate through potential crises with confidence, preserving their reputation and strengthening their relationship with their audience.

Chapter 8: Post-Crisis Assessment and Recovery

Evaluating the Impact of a Social Media Crisis

In today's digital age, social media has become an integral part of our daily lives, connecting people from all walks of life and providing a platform for individuals and businesses to express themselves. However, this interconnectedness also brings with it the potential for social media crises that can have a profound impact on public figures, influencers, entrepreneurs, and brands. In this subchapter, we will explore the importance of evaluating the impact of a social media crisis and discuss effective damage control tactics for public figures on various social media platforms.

Understanding the impact of a social media crisis is crucial for public relations managers, social media managers, and digital marketing managers, as it enables them to gauge the severity of the situation and develop appropriate strategies to mitigate the damage. By evaluating the impact, these professionals can identify the key stakeholders affected by the crisis, assess the extent of negative sentiment, and determine the potential consequences on the individual's or brand's reputation.

One important aspect of evaluating the impact of a social media crisis is monitoring online conversations and sentiment analysis. This involves utilizing social media listening tools to track mentions, hashtags, and keywords related to the crisis. By analyzing the tone and sentiment of these conversations, public relations managers can gain insights into public perception and adjust their crisis management strategies accordingly.

Additionally, evaluating the impact of a social media crisis involves conducting a thorough analysis of key performance indicators (KPIs). These KPIs may include engagement rates, follower growth, website traffic, and sales figures. By comparing these metrics before, during, and after the crisis, social media managers can quantify the impact of the crisis on the individual's or brand's online presence and business performance.

Furthermore, this subchapter will delve into damage control tactics for public figures on social media platforms. It will explore strategies such as issuing timely and transparent apologies, addressing concerns and criticisms directly, and leveraging influencers or brand advocates to rebuild trust and credibility. Moreover, the subchapter will emphasize the importance of consistent communication, active listening, and community engagement in overcoming a social media crisis.

In conclusion, understanding the impact of a social media crisis and implementing effective damage control tactics are vital for public figures, influencers, entrepreneurs, and brands. By evaluating the impact, professionals in public relations, social media management, and digital marketing can develop strategies to mitigate the damage, rebuild trust, and protect the reputation of the individual or brand in the face of a social media crisis.

Rebuilding Trust and Reputational Damage Control

In the age of social media, public figures are more vulnerable than ever before to reputational damage. A single misstep or controversial statement can quickly spread like wildfire, tarnishing their image and undermining the trust of their audience. As public relations managers, social media managers, influencers, entrepreneurs, and digital marketing managers, it is crucial to understand the strategies and tactics for rebuilding trust and engaging in effective reputational damage control.

When faced with a social media crisis, one of the first steps is to assess the situation and the extent of the damage. This involves monitoring and analyzing conversations and sentiment on various social media platforms. By understanding the public's perception, you can tailor your response and determine the best course of action to regain trust and rebuild your client's reputation.

Next, it is essential to acknowledge the issue and take responsibility. Public figures must address the crisis head-on, admitting any mistakes or misjudgments they may have made. This shows accountability and a willingness to rectify the situation. By being transparent and authentic, public figures can start rebuilding trust and showing their audience that they are committed to resolving the issue at hand.

Another crucial aspect of reputational damage control is effective communication. Public relations managers and social media managers must craft a carefully planned response strategy. This includes creating a crisis communication plan that outlines key messages, identifies the appropriate platforms for communication, and designates spokespersons or influencers who will deliver the message. Consistency in messaging and timely responses are vital to regain control of the narrative and rebuild trust.

In addition to communication strategies, it is also important to engage with the audience and stakeholders. This involves actively listening and responding to concerns, questions, and criticisms. Public figures should demonstrate empathy, understanding, and a genuine desire to address the issues raised. By engaging in open and honest dialogue, they can rebuild trust and demonstrate their commitment to making amends.

Lastly, it is crucial for public figures to learn from the crisis and implement measures to prevent future incidents. This may involve reviewing social media policies, providing training for the client's team, or partnering with experts in crisis management. By demonstrating a proactive approach to preventing similar situations, public figures can rebuild trust and reassure their audience that they are committed to avoiding future mistakes.

In conclusion, reputational damage control is a critical skill for public relations managers, social media managers, influencers, entrepreneurs, and digital marketing managers. By implementing effective strategies such as assessing the situation, taking responsibility, communicating effectively, engaging with the audience, and implementing preventive measures, public figures can rebuild trust and restore their reputation in the face of social media crises.

Implementing Long-term Strategies for Crisis Prevention

In the fast-paced digital age, public figures are constantly under scrutiny on social media platforms. One wrong move or a poorly worded post can quickly escalate into a full-blown crisis, tarnishing reputations and damaging careers. As public relations managers, social media managers, influencers, entrepreneurs, and digital marketing managers, it is crucial to be equipped with effective long-term strategies for crisis prevention and damage control.

The first step in crisis prevention is to establish a strong online presence. Building a positive and authentic personal brand across various social media platforms helps to create a solid foundation of trust with your audience. This involves consistently sharing valuable content, engaging with followers, and responding to comments and messages promptly. By being proactive in cultivating a positive image, you can significantly reduce the likelihood of a crisis.

Regularly monitoring social media platforms is another essential aspect of crisis prevention. Public figures should keep a close eye on their mentions, tags, and comments to identify any potential issues before they escalate. Utilizing social media listening tools and setting up keyword alerts can help in early detection of negative sentiment or controversial discussions surrounding your brand or persona.

Being transparent and accountable is key when it comes to crisis prevention. Public figures should take responsibility for their actions, promptly address any concerns or controversies, and provide honest and open communication with their audience. This level of transparency helps to build trust and credibility, diffusing potential crises before they spiral out of control.

Collaborating with a crisis management team is essential for public figures. By having a team of professionals who specialize in crisis communication and social media management, public figures can ensure they have a plan in place for handling crises effectively. This team can help create guidelines and protocols to follow during a crisis, ensuring consistent messaging and a coordinated response.

Lastly, continuous education and staying updated on the latest trends and best practices in social media crisis management is crucial. The digital landscape is ever-evolving, and public figures need to adapt their strategies to stay ahead of potential crises. Attending workshops, conferences, and staying connected with industry experts can provide valuable insights and help refine crisis prevention strategies.

In conclusion, implementing long-term strategies for crisis prevention is a vital aspect of managing the online presence of public figures. By establishing a strong online presence, regularly monitoring social media platforms, being transparent and accountable, collaborating with a crisis management team, and staying educated on the latest trends, public figures can effectively mitigate the risk of crises and maintain a positive reputation on social media platforms.

Continual Monitoring and Adaptation for Future Crises

In today's digital age, where social media platforms serve as a powerful tool for communication and influence, public figures face unique challenges when it comes to managing crises. The fast-paced nature of social media can amplify any negative situation, making it crucial for public figures to adopt effective damage control tactics to protect their reputation and maintain public trust.

This subchapter, "Continual Monitoring and Adaptation for Future Crises," aims to provide public relations managers, social media managers, influencers, entrepreneurs, and digital marketing managers with valuable strategies to handle crises on social media platforms. By implementing proactive measures and staying ahead of potential crises, public figures can effectively manage their online presence and mitigate damage.

The first step in this process is continual monitoring. Public figures must establish a robust monitoring system that allows them to stay informed about conversations and trends surrounding their brand or persona. By employing social media listening tools and monitoring keywords, hashtags, and mentions, public figures can quickly identify and address potential crises before they escalate. This subchapter will provide detailed insights into the best practices for setting up and utilizing monitoring systems effectively.

Furthermore, this subchapter emphasizes the importance of adapting strategies for future crises. Social media landscapes are ever-evolving, and public figures must be prepared to adjust their crisis management tactics accordingly. By studying past crisis scenarios, understanding their impact, and analyzing the response strategies employed, public figures can learn valuable lessons and improve their crisis management techniques. The content will offer practical guidance on how to evaluate and refine crisis management strategies to ensure they remain effective in the face of future challenges.

In conclusion, "Continual Monitoring and Adaptation for Future Crises" is a subchapter that serves as a comprehensive guide for public figures seeking to navigate the complex world of social media crisis management. By implementing continual monitoring and adaptation strategies, public relations managers, social media managers, and influencers can effectively control and mitigate damage to their reputation. This subchapter is an essential resource for anyone involved in managing the online presence of public figures, providing valuable insights and techniques to handle crises on social media platforms.

Chapter 9: The Role of Public Relations Managers, Social Media Managers, and Influencers

Collaborating with PR Managers for Effective Crisis Management

In the fast-paced digital age, the importance of effective crisis management for public figures cannot be overstated. With social media platforms serving as powerful tools for communication and influence, it has become imperative for public figures to be prepared for potential crises that may arise. In this subchapter, we will explore the significance of collaborating with PR managers for effective crisis management and the damage control tactics that can be employed on social media platforms.

Public relations managers play a crucial role in navigating the complex landscape of crisis management. Their expertise in strategic communication, crisis response, and media relations is invaluable when it comes to mitigating the potential damage caused by a crisis. By working closely with PR managers, public figures can develop a comprehensive crisis management plan that addresses potential risks and outlines appropriate responses.

One of the key aspects of collaborating with PR managers is the development of a crisis communication strategy. This involves identifying potential crises, establishing communication channels, and drafting key messages to be disseminated during a crisis. PR managers can help public figures craft messages that are clear, concise, and empathetic, ensuring that the right tone is struck to maintain public trust.

In the realm of social media, crisis management takes on a unique dimension. Social media managers and influencers have a critical role to play in monitoring online conversations, identifying potential crises, and responding promptly. By collaborating with PR managers, social media managers can align their efforts with the broader crisis management plan, ensuring a coordinated response across all digital platforms.

Entrepreneurs and digital marketing managers can also benefit from collaborating with PR managers during a crisis. By understanding the potential impact of a crisis on their brand reputation and customer perception, entrepreneurs can work with PR managers to develop strategies that protect their business interests. Digital marketing managers, on the other hand, can leverage their expertise in online advertising and content creation to support the crisis management efforts and maintain a positive brand image.

Damage control tactics for public figures on social media platforms are multifaceted. From issuing prompt apologies and taking responsibility to addressing concerns directly and transparently, PR managers can guide public figures in navigating the complexities of social media crises. By closely monitoring online conversations, PR managers can identify influential voices and engage with them to manage the narrative surrounding the crisis.

In conclusion, collaborating with PR managers is essential for public figures, social media managers, influencers, entrepreneurs, and digital marketing managers to effectively manage crises on social media platforms. By working together, these professionals can develop comprehensive crisis management strategies, implement damage control tactics, and safeguard the reputation and trust of public figures in the digital age.

Leveraging the Expertise of Social Media Managers

In the fast-paced world of social media, public figures are constantly exposed to the risk of online crises that can damage their reputation and impact their personal and professional lives. To effectively navigate this challenging landscape, it is crucial for public figures to have a solid understanding of damage control tactics specifically tailored for social media platforms. This subchapter explores the invaluable role of social media managers in the process of crisis management, providing insights and strategies for public figures, public relations managers, social media managers, influencers, entrepreneurs, and digital marketing managers.

Social media managers are the experts who possess the skills and knowledge necessary to handle online crises with finesse. They are adept at monitoring social media platforms, identifying potential issues, and swiftly responding to negative comments or situations before they escalate. By leveraging the expertise of social media managers, public figures can effectively manage their online presence during a crisis and minimize the impact on their brand.

One key aspect of social media crisis management is pre-planning. Social media managers can work closely with public figures to develop a comprehensive crisis management plan that outlines potential risks, identifies an appropriate response strategy, and establishes clear guidelines for communication during a crisis. This proactive approach enables public figures to be prepared for any eventuality and respond swiftly and effectively.

Additionally, social media managers play a vital role in monitoring and analyzing social media conversations surrounding public figures. By keeping a finger on the pulse of public sentiment, they can identify emerging trends, potential issues, and opportunities for engagement. This real-time monitoring allows public figures to address concerns promptly, demonstrate their transparency, and rebuild trust with their audience.

Furthermore, social media managers excel in crafting and disseminating strategic messaging during a crisis. They possess the ability to develop impactful content that resonates with the target audience and effectively communicates the public figure's perspective. Social media managers can also leverage their expertise in utilizing various social media platforms to ensure that the crisis response reaches the widest possible audience, while carefully managing the tone and timing of communication.

In conclusion, the expertise of social media managers is indispensable when it comes to effectively managing online crises for public figures. By collaborating closely with these professionals, public figures can navigate the complex world of social media with confidence, ensuring that their reputation remains intact even in the face of adversity. This subchapter provides valuable insights and strategies that will empower public relations managers, social media managers, influencers, entrepreneurs, and digital marketing managers to leverage the expertise of social media managers and successfully implement damage control tactics on social media platforms.

Harnessing the Power of Influencers during Crises

In today's digital age, social media has become a powerful tool for public figures to connect with their audience and build their personal brand. However, with great power comes great responsibility, and managing a crisis on social media platforms can be a daunting task. Public relations managers, social media managers, and influencers, entrepreneurs, and digital marketing managers alike must be equipped with effective damage control tactics to navigate through these challenging times.

One strategy that has proven to be highly effective in crisis management is harnessing the power of influencers. Influencers are individuals who have built a loyal following on social media platforms and have the ability to sway public opinion. By leveraging the influence of these individuals, public figures can regain control of the narrative and mitigate the damage caused by a crisis.

The first step in harnessing the power of influencers during a crisis is to identify the right influencers to partner with. Public relations managers and social media managers must conduct thorough research to find influencers who align with the public figure's values, target audience, and niche. It is crucial to choose influencers who have credibility and a strong following, as their endorsement can greatly impact public perception.

Once the influencers have been identified, it is essential to establish a genuine and authentic relationship with them. Public figures should approach influencers with transparency and honesty, explaining the situation and seeking their support. This collaboration should be mutually beneficial, with both parties working together to address the crisis and rebuild trust with the audience.

Influencers can play a crucial role in crisis management by sharing positive stories, testimonials, or endorsements about the public figure. Their influence can help counteract negative narratives and provide a balanced perspective to the audience. Public relations managers and social media managers should provide influencers with all the necessary information and resources to accurately convey the desired message.

Furthermore, public figures should actively engage with influencers' content during a crisis. By liking, commenting, and sharing influencers' posts, public figures show their support and appreciation, further strengthening the relationship and the impact of the collaboration.

In conclusion, harnessing the power of influencers during crises is a highly effective strategy for public figures to regain control of the narrative and mitigate damage on social media platforms. Public relations managers, social media managers, and influencers, entrepreneurs, and digital marketing managers must work together to identify the right influencers, establish genuine relationships, and collaborate on crafting a positive message. By leveraging the influence of these individuals, public figures can successfully navigate through crises and rebuild trust with their audience.

Chapter 10: Conclusion

Recap of Key Strategies and Best Practices

In the fast-paced digital era we live in, managing a crisis on social media platforms has become a crucial skill for public figures. Whether you are a celebrity, politician, or business leader, the potential for a social media crisis to erupt is always present. In this subchapter, we will recap the key strategies and best practices to effectively handle such situations and minimize damage to your reputation.

1. Be Vigilant and Monitor Social Media Channels:
As a public figure, it is essential to stay vigilant and monitor your social media channels regularly. By actively listening to conversations, you can identify potential crises before they escalate. This proactive approach allows you to respond swiftly and effectively.

2. Develop a Crisis Communication Plan:
Having a well-defined crisis communication plan is crucial. This plan should outline the steps to be taken during a crisis, key messaging, and designated spokespersons. By preparing in advance, you will be better equipped to handle any situation that arises.

3. Respond Promptly and Transparently:
In the world of social media, timeliness is crucial. When a crisis arises, respond promptly and transparently. Address the issue head-on, take responsibility where necessary, and provide updates as the situation unfolds. This approach builds trust and demonstrates accountability.

4. Engage with Your Audience:
During a crisis, it is important to maintain open lines of communication with your audience. Engage with them by responding to their comments, acknowledging their concerns, and providing accurate information. This active engagement helps build a sense of community and fosters understanding.

5. Empathize and Apologize:
If mistakes were made, it is crucial to empathize with those affected and offer a sincere apology. Demonstrating empathy and taking responsibility for any wrongdoing shows humility and a commitment to making amends.

6. Learn from Past Crises:
Take the time to analyze past crises and learn from them. Identify patterns, assess what worked and what didn't, and refine your crisis management strategies accordingly. This ongoing learning process will help you become more resilient and better prepared for future challenges.

7. Collaborate with Professionals:
Consider partnering with public relations managers, social media managers, and digital marketing experts who specialize in crisis management. Their expertise and experience can provide invaluable guidance during difficult times.

In conclusion, effectively managing a social media crisis is an essential skill for public figures. By implementing these key strategies and best practices, you can navigate through crises with confidence, minimize damage to your reputation, and emerge stronger than before. Remember, being proactive, transparent, and responsive will help you regain trust and maintain a positive online presence.

Looking Ahead: Future Trends in Social Media Crisis Management

As the digital landscape continues to evolve at a rapid pace, it is crucial for public figures to stay ahead of the game when it comes to managing crises on social media platforms. In this subchapter, we will explore the future trends in social media crisis management and equip public relations managers, social media managers, influencers, entrepreneurs, and digital marketing managers with the necessary knowledge and strategies to handle potential crises effectively.

One of the emerging trends in social media crisis management is the integration of artificial intelligence (AI) and machine learning algorithms. These technologies can help public figures monitor and analyze vast amounts of data in real-time, allowing them to identify potential crises before they escalate. AI-powered sentiment analysis tools can detect negative sentiment and alert PR managers or social media managers to take immediate action. Additionally, chatbots and virtual assistants can provide instant responses to inquiries and complaints, offering a more efficient and personalized crisis management experience.

Another trend to watch out for is the increasing importance of proactive crisis management. Public figures should no longer wait for a crisis to occur before implementing damage control tactics. Instead, they should be proactive in monitoring and managing their online presence, building strong relationships with their audience, and addressing potential issues before they become full-blown crises. This approach involves regularly monitoring social media platforms, engaging with followers, and staying updated with emerging trends, allowing public figures to mitigate risks and maintain a positive online reputation.

Furthermore, the rise of augmented reality (AR) and virtual reality (VR) technologies presents new opportunities for crisis management. Public figures can use AR/VR to create immersive experiences that effectively communicate their messages and control narratives during a crisis. By leveraging these technologies, public figures can engage with their audience in a more impactful and memorable way, fostering empathy and understanding.

Lastly, the future of social media crisis management lies in effective collaboration and coordination among different stakeholders. Public relations managers, social media managers, influencers, entrepreneurs, and digital marketing managers need to work together, leveraging their expertise and resources, to develop comprehensive crisis management strategies. This collaborative approach ensures a cohesive response to crises, minimizing the potential damage and maximizing the opportunities for recovery.

In conclusion, staying ahead of the curve in social media crisis management is essential for public figures to protect their online reputation and maintain credibility. By embracing future trends such as AI and machine learning, proactive crisis management, AR/VR technologies, and collaborative approaches, public figures can effectively navigate the ever-changing digital landscape and emerge stronger from any potential crisis.

Final Thoughts and Closing Remarks

In the rapidly evolving digital age, social media has become an integral part of our daily lives. For public figures, navigating through the vast landscape of social media platforms can be a double-edged sword. While it offers immense opportunities for engagement and influence, it also poses significant risks that can lead to reputation damage and public relations crises.

Throughout this book, we have explored the crucial strategies and tactics required to effectively manage social media crises for public figures. We have delved into the intricacies of damage control, highlighting the importance of proactive planning, swift response, and transparent communication. Now, as we conclude this subchapter, let us reflect on the key takeaways and final thoughts that can help public relations managers, social media managers, influencers, entrepreneurs, and digital marketing managers navigate the challenges of social media crisis management.

First and foremost, it is essential to acknowledge the power of social media and its impact on public perception. Public figures must recognize the potential risks and be prepared to respond swiftly and effectively to any crisis that arises. By developing a comprehensive crisis communication plan, including pre-drafted statements and a designated crisis team, you can ensure a proactive approach to managing social media crises.

Moreover, embracing transparency and authenticity is paramount. Public figures should strive to establish genuine connections with their audience, responding to criticism or negative feedback with empathy and openness.

Building a strong online presence based on trust and credibility can help mitigate the damage caused by potential crises.

Furthermore, it is crucial to monitor social media platforms diligently. By actively listening to conversations and utilizing social media listening tools, public figures can identify brewing crises early on and take appropriate action to control the narrative. Regularly analyzing engagement metrics, sentiment analysis, and trending topics can provide valuable insights into audience perceptions and help tailor crisis responses accordingly.

Lastly, public figures must understand the significance of collaboration and building strong relationships with their internal teams and external stakeholders. Establishing a crisis response team comprising skilled professionals from public relations, social media, and legal departments can ensure a coordinated and efficient response in times of crisis. Additionally, fostering relationships with key influencers, media personnel, and industry experts can offer support and amplify positive messaging during turbulent times.

In conclusion, social media crisis management for public figures demands strategic planning, swift action, and transparent communication. By implementing the damage control tactics explored in this book, public relations managers, social media managers, influencers, entrepreneurs, and digital marketing managers can effectively navigate the challenges posed by social media platforms. Remember, your reputation is your most valuable asset, and by adopting proactive measures, you can safeguard it from potential crises and emerge stronger than ever in the digital realm.

www.ingramcontent.com/pod-product-compliance
Lightning Source LLC
Chambersburg PA
CBHW060210260726

48658CB00005BA/1976